Franklin
Delano
Roosevelt

By Bonnie J. Hinman

 **Wright Group**

The McGraw·Hill Companies

www.WrightGroup.com

 **Wright Group**

Contents

Historical Time Line

Franklin D. Roosevelt lived through some perilous times in America's history. A terrible economic depression hit the nation and World War II raged, but progress never stopped. The Wright brothers made the first airplane flight, and women gained the right to vote. Teddy bears made their first appearance in 1902, supposedly named after President Theodore Roosevelt. In spite of the problems, it was an exciting time to be an American. Look below to see what other progress was made during Roosevelt's lifetime.

On January 30, Franklin Delano Roosevelt is born.

Roosevelt attends Groton prep school.

Roosevelt graduates from Harvard.

Roosevelt is elected to the New York Senate.

1882 **1896–1900** **1903** **1910**

1886 **1902** **1905**

Roosevelt marries Anna Eleanor Roosevelt.

The Statue of Liberty is dedicated.

The first teddy bears are made.

The Boy Scouts of America is founded.

Orville and Wilbur Wright make the first successful powered airplane flight.

All American women get the right to vote after the 19th Amendment is ratified.

World WarI begins.

Winnie the Pooh by A.A. Milne is first published.

Roosevelt runs for vice president, but loses.

Roosevelt is elected president of the United States. He would be reelected three times.

On April 12, Roosevelt suddenly dies.

1914 — **1920** — **1926** **1932** — **1945**
— **1918** **1921** **1928** **1941**

Roosevelt contracts polio.

Roosevelt is elected governor of New York.

World War I ends.

Mickey Mouse first appears in the *Steamboat Willie* cartoon.

Japanese planes bomb Pearl Harbor, and World War II begins.

Author's Note

Franklin Delano Roosevelt, also known as FDR, was an active man who loved to hike and sail and play games before he contracted polio. He loved people and eagerly visited every part of a district or state when he campaigned for office. He used his energy to help the American people in many ways while he was president.

The years when Roosevelt was president were difficult ones as the Depression and World War ll swept over our country. I admire Roosevelt's can-do attitude. If one possible solution didn't work, he was ready to try another. He never gave up.

One of Roosevelt's toughest jobs while he was president was convincing Congress and American citizens that the U.S. must help Great Britain and France in World War II. Roosevelt believed that America must help our allies fight against Adolph Hitler. He showed great determination and persuaded Congress to send supplies. Those supplies helped Great Britain survive and gave America's factory workers jobs.

Roosevelt didn't listen to critics who said we should stay out of the war in Europe. He did what he thought was right and the war was won. Because of this and his many other contributions to American life, Franklin Delano Roosevelt is truly an Amazing American.

Bonnie J. Hinman

CHAPTER ONE

Living with Polio

Franklin Delano Roosevelt, his wife Eleanor, and their five children vacationed on Campobello Island, off New Brunswick, Canada in August of 1921. This was Roosevelt's first real vacation in over ten years, and he was happy for the break. The day began like any other. Roosevelt took his three older children—Anna, James, and Elliot—for a sail. After an hour or so, they spotted a small fire on a nearby island and worked excitedly to put it out. Then they sailed home so that Roosevelt could get in a two-mile run and a quick swim before dinner.

Back from his swim, Roosevelt was exhausted—too tired to change out of his bathing suit. When he went to bed before supper, his wife, Eleanor, knew something was wrong.

The Roosevelts' Campobello Island cottage

Roosevelt's favorite sport was swimming.

By the next morning, Roosevelt's temperature was 102 degrees. By the end of that day, his legs, neck, and back were aching painfully. He couldn't move his legs at all.

After two doctors examined and misdiagnosed Roosevelt, Dr. Robert Lovett finally figured out what was wrong. Roosevelt had contracted a virus several weeks before his visit to Campobello. The virus would leave him paralyzed from the waist down for the rest of his life. Roosevelt had contracted polio.

Did You Know... Photographers who covered the president had a gentleman's agreement not to take pictures of Roosevelt in his wheelchair. In that time, a physically challenged person wasn't always considered to have the same abilities as someone who wasn't physically challenged.

Back home in New York, Roosevelt worked hard to overcome his illness. He was determined to walk again, and for the next seven years, he tried his best. He attempted to walk with crutches and his legs bound in heavy steel **braces**. One day, he became determined to walk

Roosevelt chats with the daughter of a friend.

the quarter-mile from his home to his driveway. Day after day he tried, working up a great sweat and happily chatting with whoever helped him along. While he once made it halfway to the driveway, he never reached his goal. And he would never again walk without assistance.

For the rest of his life, Roosevelt tried to find ways to overcome polio. He took special baths, massages, and met with many doctors and therapists. Through it all, however, his spirits remained high, and he refused to be limited by what many considered a disability.

Roosevelt (far right) bathes at Warm Springs, Georgia.

Leap Back in Time

Franklin D. Roosevelt led our nation during one of the most difficult periods in American history—the Great Depression and World War II. During the Depression, the economy took a huge downturn, leading to the loss of many occupations. Businessmen, once well off, now found themselves waiting in line for soup and bread. People sold anything they owned on street corners, trying to make money. A demand for women in the workforce arose when men were called to fight in World War II. How do you think people living during these times got through their economic and occupational struggles?

EMPLOYMENT LINE

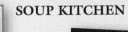

SOUP KITCHEN

STREET CORNER VENDING

POSTER SOLICITING
WORK FOR WOMEN

SKYSCRAPER
CONSTRUCTION
PROJECT

CHAPTER TWO

The Roosevelts

Franklin Delano Roosevelt was born on January 30, 1882, at Springwood, the family home in Hyde Park, New York. He was an only child, and his parents took him everywhere with them.

Franklin loved to be outdoors and spent much of his time fishing and wandering around his father's land. Franklin's father taught him to ride a horse, shoot guns, and handle boats. He loved sailing, and his favorite childhood stories were pirate adventures.

Young Franklin on the shoulder of his father

The Roosevelt mansion in Hyde Park, New York

Like most boys from wealthy families, Franklin was tutored at home. He learned French and German and loved to read. When he was 14, Franklin went to boarding school in Massachusetts. Groton School was a big change for him, but he adjusted to the new rules. After four years at Groton, Franklin went to Harvard University.

Young Franklin with his mother

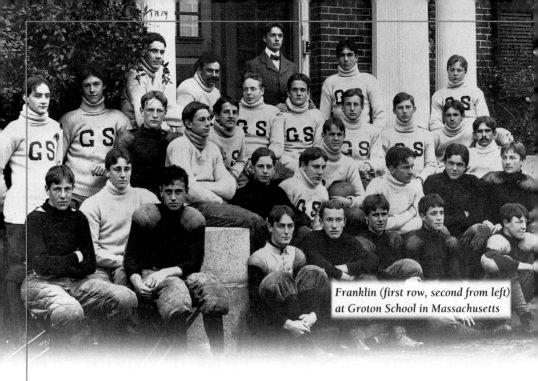

Franklin (first row, second from left) at Groton School in Massachusetts

Franklin did reasonably well at Harvard, studying history and politics, and even writing for the school newspaper. But he was more interested in sports than his studies, and his grades were not as strong as they could have been.

In Their Own Words

"**I am getting on very well and so far I have not had any warnings, latenesses, or marks.**"

~From a letter Franklin wrote to his parents during his first month at Groton

Theodore Roosevelt

While at Harvard, Franklin became engaged to Anna Eleanor Roosevelt, his fifth cousin. Eleanor was the niece of Theodore Roosevelt, the current president of the United States. Franklin admired Theodore very much and sometimes went to the White House for visits. Theodore stood in for Eleanor's father when she and Franklin were married on March 17, 1905.

Franklin and Eleanor when they were a young couple

Roosevelt as a New York state senator

The next years were busy for the Roosevelts. Franklin was a lawyer with a successful practice. He and Eleanor had six children, but one died when he was eight months old. As his children grew older, Franklin took them sailing and horseback riding, much like his own father had done with him.

In 1910, Roosevelt ran for the New York senate on the Democratic ticket. He was following Theodore Roosevelt's political footsteps. He won the election and would serve as a senator for the next three years.

Roosevelt and Eleanor with their first two children in 1908

In 1913, Roosevelt was appointed assistant secretary of the navy. This was a very important job and meant Roosevelt would meet many influential people in the political world. His political career was off to a great start.

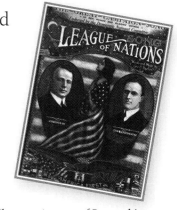

Sheet music cover of Roosevelt's 1920 campaign song

Roosevelt (right) and James M. Cox campaigning in 1920

In 1920, the Democratic Party nominated Roosevelt for vice president of the United States. The Democratic presidential candidate was James M. Cox. The Democrats lost the election, but Roosevelt gained national attention.

In Their Own Words

"I get my fingers into everything and there's no law against it."

~Franklin Roosevelt speaking of his job as assistant secretary of the navy in 1913

CHAPTER THREE

Hard Times

After the 1920 election, Roosevelt became vice president of the Fidelity and Deposit Company of Maryland. In the summer of 1921, he took a vacation with his family. They enjoyed a pleasant summer until Roosevelt contracted polio.

In 1927, after years of trying to overcome the disease, Roosevelt established the Georgia Warm Springs Foundation in Warm Springs, Georgia. There, others living with polio could soothe their limbs in warm mineral water baths.

The Georgia Warm Springs Foundation

In 1928, Roosevelt was asked to run for governor of New York. He wasn't sure he was ready to enter politics again, but Eleanor encouraged him. Worried that people would not

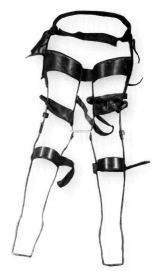

These leg braces were worn by Franklin Roosevelt.

vote for him if they saw him in a wheelchair, Roosevelt did most of his campaigning standing up. He wore leg braces and was often held up by assistants. Later that year, he won the election.

Governor Franklin Roosevelt

In Their Own Words

"But a governor does not have to be an acrobat. We do not elect him for his ability to do a double back-flip or a handspring. The work of the governorship is brainwork."

~Alfred Smith, former governor of New York, speaking in 1928 about Roosevelt

In 1929, the **stock market** collapsed and many people lost their money. America plunged into the **Great Depression**. Workers lost their jobs and children went hungry. Roosevelt worked hard to help the people of New York. The next year, he was reelected governor by a landslide.

Long lines at a soup kitchen

Migrant Mother, *a famous depression-era picture taken by Dorothea Lange*

Roosevelt gained some good experience as governor. In 1932, with firm backing from New York Democrats, Roosevelt was nominated for president.

Franklin Roosevelt campaign button

Roosevelt promised to strengthen the economy and help rebuild confidence in banks and other financial institutions. He also wanted to create new jobs and help struggling farmers. His plan became known as the "New Deal," and it appealed to the American people. Roosevelt was elected 32nd President of the United States.

Roosevelt and vice presidential candidate John Garner

Did You Know...

The many agencies that Roosevelt established during the Depression were sometimes called the Alphabet Soup Agencies, for example:
- CCC – Civilian Conservation Corps
- FERA – Federal Emergency Relief Administration
- TVA – Tennessee Valley Authority
- WPA – Works Progress Administration

Roosevelt took the oath of office, March 4, 1933.

By the time he gave his **inaugural address** in March, 1933, the Great Depression was at its lowest point. Americans were afraid of what the future held. But in his speech, Roosevelt

Roosevelt gives one of his "fireside chats"

reminded them that "the only thing we have to fear is fear itself." In his first hundred days as president, Roosevelt sent a flood of **bills** to Congress that provided money to feed the hungry and jobs for the unemployed.

Did You Know...

Secretary of Labor Frances Perkins, appointed by President Roosevelt, was the first woman to serve on a presidential cabinet.

Alf Landon

Not everyone agreed with Roosevelt's New Deal. Alf Landon, the 1936 Republican presidential candidate, thought the New Deal hurt American businesses and involved too much government spending. On the other hand, Huey Long, a U.S. Senator from Louisiana, said that Roosevelt hadn't gone far enough to help the poor. He wanted to guarantee every family a certain income, which he thought would do away with poverty.

During this time, Roosevelt made radio speeches called "fireside chats." He talked to people as if they were sitting around the fire in his living room. He discussed the problems facing the nation and how he planned to resolve them. Americans listened to their new president and felt hopeful for the first time in many months.

WPA (Works Progress Administration) workers clear flood debris.

CHAPTER FOUR

War Comes

*I*n 1936, Roosevelt was reelected president. Three years later, the depression raged on and war had broken out in Europe. German **dictator** Adolph Hitler was trying to conquer Europe. Italy's dictator, Benito Mussolini, joined forces with Hitler. On September 3, 1939, Great Britain and France declared war on Germany. Roosevelt wanted to help Britain and France, but most Americans wanted to stay out of the war.

German troops enter Paris on June 14, 1940.

An ammunition plant worker during World War II

However, Roosevelt believed that the outcome of war in Europe could threaten the American way of life if the United States didn't get involved. He knew that Hitler and Mussolini held beliefs that were very different from the American ideals of life, liberty, and the pursuit of happiness. He finally convinced Congress to send war supplies to Great Britain and France. American factories ran day and night, building planes and making ammunition. This helped improve the economy and eventually brought the Great Depression to an end.

In Their Own Words

"Franklin Roosevelt is the best friend Britain ever had."

~Winston Churchill, prime minister of Great Britain during most of World War II

While war raged in Europe, Asian nations were also in conflict. Japan was trying to take over China. The United States sided with China, offering support and cutting off ties with Japan. On December 7, 1941, a date Roosevelt declared would "live in infamy," Japanese planes attacked **Pearl Harbor** in Hawaii. Four days later, Japan's ally, Germany declared war on the United States. World War II had come to America.

Roosevelt signs the Declaration of War in 1941.

Counterpoint

Charles Lindbergh

Famous aviator Charles Lindbergh disagreed very strongly with Roosevelt or any person who wanted America to help Great Britain and France in their war against Germany. He made many speeches against war, and in one he said, "The destiny of this country does not call for our involvement in European wars." He claimed that Roosevelt was trying to drive America into a war that could not be won.

On December 7, 1941, the battleship California sinks after being bombed.

In the next years, America and its allies battled Japan, Germany, and Italy. The war was difficult on Roosevelt, too. He was exhausted from traveling all over the world for conferences and meetings. In 1942, 26 nations united against Germany, Italy, and Japan. Roosevelt called them the United Nations. Their mission was to work toward international peace and prosperity.

In Their Own Words

"We don't like it—we did not want to get in it—but we are in it, and we are going to fight it with everything we have got."

~Franklin Delano Roosevelt, speaking shortly after the United States entered World War II in 1941

Roosevelt driving with his dog in 1944

Sadly, Roosevelt would not live to see the end of World War II or the first official meeting of the United Nations. In 1944, he became president for the fourth time. Many people thought he looked thin, pale, and old. A medical examination revealed that he had serious heart problems. Doctors placed him on a strict diet and gave him medicine, but they could do little about the stress he was under.

Did You Know... Roosevelt loved dogs and took his Scottish terrier, Fala, with him whenever he could. The Franklin D. Roosevelt Memorial in Washington, D.C. has a statue of Fala sitting near Roosevelt.

Mourners pay their last respects at Roosevelt's burial in Hyde Park, New York.

In April, Roosevelt managed to get away to Georgia for a vacation. After a week of rest, he looked better. On April 12, while posing for a portrait, Roosevelt complained of a terrible headache. Shortly thereafter, he slumped in his chair and passed out. He died two hours later of a massive stroke. He was 63 years old.

Roosevelt's sudden death makes the front page of newspapers.

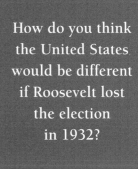

How do you think the United States would be different if Roosevelt lost the election in 1932?

Conclusion

The president's sudden death made everyone in America sad. People stood on the street and cried when they heard the news.

On his desk, Roosevelt left a speech he'd been writing. In it he wrote, "The only limit to our realization of tomorrow will be our doubts of today. Let us move forward with strong and active faith."

Franklin Delano Roosevelt moved forward strongly throughout his life. Polio didn't stop him and neither did the Great Depression or World War II. Throughout his life, Roosevelt's spirit never failed him or the nation he served.

Roosevelt and Fala statues in Washington, D.C.

Glossary

bills proposed laws which are sent to the legislature for a vote

braces heavy metal supports that go around a person's legs or other part of the body

dictator one person who has complete control over an entire country

Great Depression the ten years after the stock market crashed in 1929 when factories and businesses closed, leaving millions of Americans without jobs

inaugural address the first public speech given by an elected president

Pearl Harbor a U.S. navy base on the south side of Oahu, Hawaii

stock market the business carried on at the stock exchange where stocks and bonds are bought and sold

Index